LYNNE MILLER
AND CAROLE BATTEN

SHORT-
SPAN
ACTIVITIES

*Ideas
for Utilizing
Spare Minutes
in the Classroom*

Citation Press   New York   1973

THIRD PRINTING

Cover design by SPRING

Printed in the U.S.A.

Contents

Note to the Teacher

The ideas for *Short-Span Activities* grew out of our own teaching experience. We found that even with the best lesson plans there were many times when a source book of quick activities would have been immensely helpful. There is always an unexpected five or ten minutes when assembly or recess or the final bell is delayed, or when students are restless and need a quick change of pace.

This handy source book offers more than eighty games and activities for different time-spans, subject areas, and grade levels. Most of the games and activities can be adapted to your special needs. They may be presented as team or individual competition or simply as exercises, oral or written. To save time on written activities, we suggest that each child have a "free time" notebook available in his desk, and that more or less permanent teams be set up in advance.

Language Arts

Word Usage

Come to Compound Country

Write several compound words on the board. Have the children draw pictures to show that they understand the meaning.

> *Example:* Boardwalk, popcorn, footbridge, toenail, windmill

Word Searching

Write a fairly long word on the board, and have the children write down all the words they can find in the word. The child with the most words wins.

> *Example:* American—hidden words:
>
> | | | |
> |------|-------|------|
> | man | mica | rice |
> | can | cane | an |
> | name | ram | mare |
> | ran | crane | nice |
> | Eric | ice | mean |

Blends

When you say "go," the children write as many words as they can think of starting with a blend such as "dr."

> *Example:* draw
> drum
> drown

Other 2-letter blends: bl, cl, cr, br, tr, fr, gr, fl, gl, dr, pl, pr, sl, sm, sn, sp, sk, st, sw.

Rhymes

Many children are intrigued with rhyming words. Instruct the children to write as many words as they can think of that rhyme with a given word.

> *Example:* BOOK
> look
> crook
> took

(As with other games, a winner may be picked if desired.)

Newspaper Reporting

Have the children invent newspaper headlines (phrases that announce a news item). You may set limits to the number of words they can use in each one.

Example: 2-word headline: WAR ENDS
3-word headline: NEW SCHOOL HOLIDAY
4-word headline: HOTTEST DAY THIS YEAR.

As a follow-up, have the children bring in funny or exciting headlines from papers.

Logical Placement

Write several sentences on the board which form an out-of-order story. The children must put the events in a logical order.

Example: The boy is scared and drops his ice cream cone.

The boy is mowing the lawn.

The boy hops on his bike and goes to the store.

The boy's father gives him a quarter.

A dog barks loudly.

Word Freedom

Begin by mentioning any word; for example, "moon." The first player repeats your word and adds the *very next* word that enters his mind. He might say "moon-sun." The next player could say "sun-daughter" and so forth until each child has had a turn. This is an excellent game to encourage ingenuity and free association.

Opposites

The first child on one team says an adjective or an adverb. He might say "best."

The first member of the opposing team must quickly give the antonym. In this case the word would be "worst." If he cannot answer correctly the one who gave the word has a chance to answer and win the point. Then the next child on the winning team gives a word.

> *Examples:* much—little
> full—empty
> able—unable

Not Quite Twins

The same game can be played asking for homonyms. A child says "here," and spells it, and an opposite team member must spell the same sounding word another way ("hear"). Or each child thinks of as many sound-alikes as he can. The child with the most words wins. Explain that most pun jokes are based on sound-alike words. ("If Mississippi wore Ohio's New Jersey, what would Delaware?")

Word Series

Write a short word on the board. Ask the first student to see if he can change one letter to make a new word. Then the next child changes one letter in *that* word. Examples: kind, find, mind. Or mine, mane, mare, maze, and so forth.

Try to get as many children as possible to contribute a word.

Add-a-Word

The first child says a word. The next child adds a word that starts with the last letter of the first word. Since the object is to make a sentence, a good beginning word would be "the" or "what."

Example: Th*e e*lephan*t t*rampe*d d*ownhill.

As soon as one sentence is finished, another one may be begun.

Your Name's Place

This game is particularly helpful in the beginning of the year to familiarize the children with each other's names. With younger children, split the class into four or five groups. Each group should form a circle, then line up alphabetically, according to their first or last names. The first group that is ready and correct wins. With older children, split the class into two teams and have each team line up alphabetically on opposite sides of the room. Or pass a complete list of the class to each child and have him number the names in alphabetical order. (Use last names and first initials.)

Alphabetical Race

Read off six to twelve like things—names of states, cities, countries, famous people, and so forth. Have the children write them down and number them in alphabetical order. The first child to get the list right wins for his team.

This may be increased in difficulty as the year progresses by giving several words that start with the same letter.

Abbreviations

Write a varied list of words on the board which have standard abbreviations (such as pound, California, Monday). Have the children write the abbreviations. Each child gets a point for each correct abbreviation. This activity should be used only after abbreviations have been studied. It may be given a theme by asking for calendar abbreviations, measurements, states, and so forth.

Similar Words

Say or write a word on the board, and have the children write as many synonyms for it as they can. Let the children use their dictionaries (if they have them). Set a time limit. If there is extra time, have the children either find opposites for each word or put them in alphabetical order.

Categories

Choose a category such as food, book titles, flowers, famous people, states, or household items. Child #1 on Team A asks Child #1 on the opposing team to think of a food beginning with the letter "p." If he can do so, he earns a point for his team. Now, the second child on Team B asks the second child on Team A to do the same thing. If a child cannot answer the given question, the opposing team earns a point. The winner's team earns the next chance to ask the question each time.

Vowel Code

Write a sentence on the board, but eliminate all vowels in the words. Let the children try to guess what the sentence says.

Example: Y cn rd wtht vwls f y wrk hrd. Smtms t's sy, smtms t's hrd! (You can read without vowels if you work hard. Sometimes it's easy, sometimes it's hard.)

Spelling

Word Throw

A child stands in front of the class and throws a bean bag (or, if not available, a soft board eraser) *underhand* to a child sitting. As he throws it, he calls out a spelling word which the catcher must spell. If the catcher spells the word correctly, it is then his turn to throw the bean bag. If the catcher cannot spell the word correctly, the thrower picks another child, throws the bean bag to the new child, repeating the word which has not yet been spelled correctly. This is repeated until a child answers with the correct spelling. He then becomes the tosser.

Ghost

This game works best when the children are sitting in circles, in groups of five or six. One student says a letter, and each player adds a letter to the letters previously said. The object of the game is to make words, trying to make the word end on someone else. Every child can be challenged by the other players after he has added his letter, if the other players doubt that the child actually is thinking of a real word. If it turns out that the child was not really thinking of a real word and the others have discovered this through challenging him, that child becomes a "G." If a child must add the last letter of a word, thus finishing the spelling of that word, the child will become a "G" also. For example, if the letters are "b-l-a-c" and it is John's turn, if John adds a "k" to end the word, he becomes a "G" and a new word is started. A child is out if he makes five mistakes, thus becoming a G-H-O-S-T. In this game, three letter words may not be used.

Baseball

The corner nearest the blackboard is home base. The other corners in the room are bases #1, #2, and #3 consecutively. Seat Teams A and B on opposite sides of the room. The first batter from Team A walks up to home plate. He is asked to spell a word taken from the current spelling list. If he does this correctly, he may walk from home plate to first base. Now the second batter on Team A steps up to home plate and he too is asked to spell a word. If he does so, he may walk to first base, and the child who is already on first will advance to second base. When a child has been to all three bases and returns to home plate, he earns a point for his team. Each time a child misspells a word, he makes an out and must return to his seat. When one team acquires three outs, it is the other team's turn to have a chance at bat. The winner is determined by the number of runs.

Hangman

Draw a noose on the board. (This may be a simple number 7 with a rope dangling from it.) Think of a word and draw blanks to represent the number of letters in that word. For instance if the word you picked is the word "ashes," you would write - - - - - on the board. The children must guess which letters are in the word. When a child guesses a correct letter, fill it in its proper place. If a child guesses a wrong letter, draw one part of a stick figure man under the noose until a whole body is completed. The parts which may be drawn on the figure are a head, a line for the body, two arms, legs, hands, feet, eyes, a nose, and a mouth. A simple stick figure works well. (To give the children more chances, ears, fingers and toes may be added.) If there are double letters in the word, both should be filled in when one is guessed. If the body is completed before the word is guessed, the teacher (or leader) wins. If the word is guessed before the body is completed, the children are the winners. The child who guesses the word first may become the "executioner" and take the teacher's place.

Unscramble Me

Write a word on the board in which the letters are not in their proper order. The children must change the letters around until a proper word is spelled.

Example: *Y I R T S H O* (history)

Spelling Be-In

The class is separated into two teams. Use the current spelling list from which to pick the words. Direct the first child on Team A to spell a certain word. If he spells it correctly, he remains standing and a new word is given to the first child on Team B. If someone misspells the word, he is out of the game, and must sit. The misspelled word is given to someone on the other team, and this continues until it is spelled correctly.

Memory

Witness

Designate one child to be the victim. The other children are witnesses. The victim goes through a series of five or six different actions. He may open and close the door, write the words "three hours and forty five seconds" on the blackboard, look suspiciously out the window, and start to count the children. To let the others know he is finished, he sits at his desk and says "I'm innocent." At this point the other children must write down all his actions—in order. The child with all items correct wins and he may be the next victim.

Sequence

This is an effective game for those periods when there are only two or three minutes in which to play. Call out a series of five or more directions such as: "Touch your toes without bending your knees, clap your hands twice under your left leg, and stand on your right foot while you count to eleven." After the directions are given, pick a volunteer to execute these actions in the order given. If he can do all the actions correctly and in order, then he may issue a series of directions and pick someone to follow them.

What Did You See?

Place eight to ten objects on a table or desk. (Try to do this when the students are not watching.) Cover the objects up. Explain to the children that you are going to reveal the objects for several seconds and that when you tell them it is time, they should write down as many of the items as they can remember. As they become more experienced, the number of objects can be increased.

Shopping

This is a good game to reinforce listening and memory skills. The first child says, "I went to the store and bought an apple."

The second child repeats what the first child has said and adds an item that begins with the letter "b." Thus, he might say, "I went to the store and bought an apple and a balloon."

The third child repeats the words of the first two, in order, and adds a word that begins with the letter "c." If a child forgets, he is out and the next child takes his turn. However, if three children in a row miss, a new game should begin.

Grandmother's Trunk

This is a more difficult version of "Shopping." It is played in exactly the same way except the items are not said in alphabetical order. Simple items (a hat, a glove) or more difficult descriptions (a black silk dress with a beaded collar) may be used; and instead of saying "I went to the store and bought," each player says, "I packed my grandmother's trunk, and in it I put . . . "

Creative Writing

If I Were Charlie Brown . . .

On the board, write the phrase "Happiness is when . . . " The children must finish the sentence. You may guide them with some examples, such as: "Happiness is when you are picked to be in an assembly," or " . . . you earn a quarter by yourself," or " . . . summer is coming."

Group Story

Invent the first sentence of a story and deliver it to the class. Each child adds a sentence or two. (He may "pass" if he has nothing to add.) For example, you may say, "Once upon a time there lived a little prince." Then the first child may add, "He lived on a desert island." The game continues until the story is completed, and a new one may begin.

Developing Descriptive Ability

Place an object in front of the class such as an eraser. Say to the class, "Let's pretend you must explain what an eraser is to a child who cannot see. How would you describe it?" Possible answers might be related to the shape (in the case of an eraser, the shape should be described as rectangular), the color (gray), the texture (like fuzzy wool cloth, hard), the weight (light).

Finish the Verse

Ask the children to choose a nursery rhyme and make up their own endings. It is not essential that the words rhyme.

> Example: Jack and Jill went up the hill
> To fetch a pail of water.
> But when they got there
> The dinner bell rang,
> So they ran back home again.

Older children may delight in finding new rhymed lines for familiar verses.

Do-It-Yourself Story

This is an individual activity. Begin a story of several sentences. You might say, "You are alone in a haunted castle. It is dark and cold. You are very hungry. But you cannot think about your stomach because you are there in the castle to search for evidence. Suddenly, you hear a loud noise." Instruct the children to write their own endings to the story.

Restaurant Owner for a Day

Tell the children to pretend they are going to be the proprietors of a big and fancy restaurant. Tell them to write down everything they will need to furnish the restaurant. They can list such things as plates, butter knives, table cloths, candles, toothpicks, and so forth.

Wishful Thinking

Tell the children that a fairy godmother has visited them and that she has granted them five wishes. Ask them to write their wishes.

Example: To build a raft and go to sea.

To eat a half-gallon of maple walnut ice cream without getting sick.

To be the first lady President of the United States.

The Best or Worst Thing That Ever Happened to Me

Instruct the children to write a paragraph describing the very best (or worst) thing that has ever happened to them.

If I Were President . . .

Ask the children to make believe that they are preparing to run for President of the United States. Have them write down three or four promises that they would make to the voters. Some examples might be to raise the salaries of postal employees, to make a law against buying guns, to set aside more land for recreation, to help states and cities fight pollution, or to create more jobs.

Pantomime

Word Pantomime

Whisper a descriptive word to a child to pantomime. You might tell the child to act tired or angry or hungry. The student acts the word out for the rest of the class. When someone guesses the word, he has a chance to think of a word and to pantomime it.

Object Pantomime

Walk around the room pretending to carry a large basket. Let the children "take" a household item from the basket and allow them to pantomime the use of their item. For example, if a child decides he has taken a stove, he may show that he can turn it on and off, open the oven, burn his hand, take out a cake. The rest of the class tries to guess what his item is.

Scene Pantomime

Whisper a pretend situation to one child. An example might be a vacuum cleaner salesman trying to sell to a housewife, a car salesman demonstrating a car, a woman buying at a grocery or butcher store, a girl fixing face and hair before a party, a woman baking a cake, or a paperboy delivering papers. The children must guess the scene and if someone guesses correctly, it is his turn to make up a situation and whisper it to a classmate, or to act one out.

Animal Actions

Warn the children that they should listen very carefully to what you are about to read. Explain that you are going to select someone to be the animal about whom you will read. Then read the following paragraph:

The wild horse stomped his left foot angrily. He looked around, bent his head down and hungrily snatched a mouthful of grass. He snorted with pleasure, and galloped off.

The child selected must then perform all the actions in the order in which they were read. The more actions given, the more difficult the game.

Social Studies Activities

Word Trains

Using countries, states, cities, or towns, begin a "word-train." One child names one of the above and the next child must name a word that begins with the last letter of the word previously said. An example using states might be: New Yor*k* — *K*ansa*s* — *S*outh Dakot*a* — *A*labam*a* — *A*rkansas. When the entire class has exhausted all the possible answers, begin a new train.

A to Z

Have the children mark the letters of the alphabet down one side of their papers. Name a category and have the children find a word for each letter of the alphabet. For example, if cities and towns are the category, one might use the following: A—Allentown, B—Boston, C—Chicago, D—Detroit. If the class is familiar with maps, this will add an exploring dimension to the game.

State Your State

Direct the children to write down as many states as they can think of. After five or ten minutes have them stop. The child with the greatest number of states wins.

Which Came First?

Write five or more historical facts on the board. Tell the children to rewrite them in the proper chronological order, beginning with the earliest event.

Example: (3) The Pilgrims landed at Plymouth Rock.
(4) George Washington crossed the Delaware.
(2) Christopher Columbus discovered America.
(5) The car was invented.
(1) Christianity was founded.

Who Works Here?

Have the students list all the people who work in an airport, a railroad station, a bus terminal, or any other large institution. For example in an airport one might find: porters, waitresses, reservation clerks, car rental agents, parking lot attendants, managers, and baggage men.

Occupations

The children may enjoy compiling a list of the numerous job opportunities in America. Set a time limit and determine the winner by the number of jobs listed. Some examples might be: doctor, garbage collector, air-traffic controller, or textile manufacturer.

So You Like to Eat ...

Tell the children to each pick a favorite restaurant, American or foreign. Then ask them to list which foods can be eaten there.

Example: In a Chinese restaurant, one may order:
> Tea
> Fortune Cookies
> Chicken Chow Mein
> Sweet and Sour Shrimp
> Moo Goo Gai Pan

What's in the Room?

Choose a room found generally in every house or apartment, and have the children list items which they know might be found in that room: kitchen, dining room, living room. Or a child can have the other children guess what room he is thinking of by naming items it might contain. This may not be as easy as it seems, since rugs, tables, and dishes are found in many rooms.

Creative Greeting Cards

Direct the children to write a short message for cards for special occasions (Christmas, Easter, and so forth). One way to do this is to take the name of the occasion and find an appropriate adjective or phrase for each letter. Here is an example for Father's Day:

> F is for fair.
> A is for attentive.
> T is for thoughtful.
> H is for helpful.
> E is for eager.
> R is for responsible.

A more creative approach to greetings is to simply let the child write whatever comes to mind. For a new baby, one might say, "Dear Parents, I'm glad you gave me a new playmate."

Sports

Have the children list as many sports as they can. The child with the longest list wins. Accept any legitimate sport, such as croquet, basketball, tennis, hockey, or racing cars.

Math Activities

Number Bee

This game is similar to a spelling bee, except that the questions are in the form of math problems. The class is divided into two teams. Questions are alternated between the teams, and children who miss are out. The winner can be determined either by the last child participating, or by the team with the most players left when the bell rings.

Magic Squares

Reproduce the following chart on the board, leaving spaces where the numbers are circled. Each row across and each row down is an addition problem. The children must fill in the empty boxes.

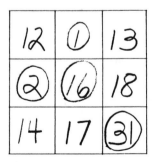

The identical game may be played by substituting subtraction problems for addition problems:

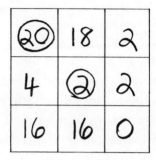

Once the children understand the concept, use more difficult numbers.

Here is a slight variation of Magic Squares, in which the addition of all three numbers in any direction (including diagonally) will result in the same total (in this case, 21).

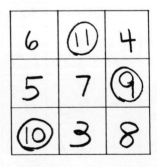

Fraction Relay

On the board, write a fraction that has not yet been reduced to its lowest terms. A child from each of the two teams calls out the fraction reduced to its lowest possible terms. The first to correctly do so earns a point for his team. Some examples you might write are 10/15, 6/8, 27/33 or 50/100.

Math Progressions

Write any of the following progressions on the board, and let the children figure out the pattern. (They may use scratch paper.)

3, 9, 27, 81, 243 (multiply by three)
1, 3, 5, 7, 9 (add three, subtract one)
2, 5, 11, 23, 47 (multiply by two and add one)

When a child discovers the pattern he may write a progression for the others to guess. Progressions may use addition, subtraction, multiplication, division, or a combination of these processes.

Multiplication Tag

Have the children form a circle. Place two or three children in the middle. One child is "it." He walks around the circle, stops behind someone, and asks that child a multiplication problem, such as 12 x 8.

If the child who is asked can give the correct answer before any of the children inside the circle can, then it is his turn to be "it." If a child on the inside of the circle answers correctly first, then the same questioner invents another problem and gives it to another child.

Quicky Quiz

Draw two boxes on the board. Write similar (but not identical) math problems in each box. Call on one child from each of two teams to do the problems at the board. The first child to solve his problems correctly wins a point for his team.

Roman Numerals

Write several Roman numerals on the board. Instruct the children to convert them to Arabic numbers, and then add them to find the sum. The first child with the correct answer wins.

The reverse may be done also. Write some Arabic numbers on the board. The child must change these into Roman numerals, again adding to find the sum. For a more difficult variation of the game, set up the problem as one of subtraction, multiplication, or division.

If you have extra time, the children may also enjoy a race to see who can write the Roman numerals one through fifty the fastest.

Buzz

Each student counts out loud when his turn comes, starting with number one. Whenever a number with a seven in it comes up, or whenever there is a number that is a multiple of seven, the player whose turn it is must say "buzz" instead of the number. (Buzz, therefore, would be substituted for the numbers 7, 14, 17, 21, 27, 28 and so forth.) When a player forgets to say "buzz," he is out.

This game may be played with other numbers such as six or eight. To increase the difficulty of the game, there may be two buzz numbers used simultaneously, such as seven and nine.

Measure for Measure

Have the children write down the missing word in the following statements. The team having the most children with the correct answers wins.

$12'' = 1$ _____ $3' = 1$ _____

60 seconds $= 1$ _____   60 minutes $= 1$ _____

8 quarts $=$ _____pints   2 quarts $=$ _____gallon

2 pints $= 1$ _____   4 quarts $= 1$ _____

6 objects $=$ _____dozen   12 objects $=$ _____dozen

90 minutes $=$ _____hours

Science Activities

Bird Brain Teaser

Tell the children to list the names of as many birds (or flowers) as they can think of. You may give them examples such as hummingbird, oriole, and woodpecker. The first child with the most comprehensive list wins. (Variations may include: naming things that a magnet will attract, things that live under water, and so forth.)

Track It to the Tree

Ask the children to name as many products as they can think of that are made from trees. Answers may be any wood product (picture frames, bow and arrow, a violin); paper products (candy wrappers); rubber products (balloons, tires); maple sugar, nuts, fruits, and so forth. The child with the most complete list wins.

What Floats?

Have the children name as many things as they can that will float in water. The child with the most correct answers wins. If you have an empty aquarium in the room, fill it with water for a demonstration of things that float and things that sink.

Ecology

Name an animal. Then ask the children to name several things that it needs in order to survive.

Example: alligator — fish, fresh water, birds

horse — space, grass, water, salt

A more advanced variation is to name a general concept, such as soil. Ask the children to think of other things which are closely related. Counterparts of soil could be rocks, earth, air, moisture.

Adaptable Games

Throughout this book, there are various activities which may be readily adapted to science if appropriate vocabulary is used.

1. *Alphabetical Race,* page 10.
2. *Word Throw,* page 12.
3. *Hangman,* page 14.
4. *Unscramble Me,* page 15.
5. *I'm Thinking of a Person* (in which plants or animals may be substituted), page 39.

Art Activities

Designs

Give each of the children a plain white sheet of bond or shelf paper. Instruct them to draw lines in all directions, from one end of the paper to the other. A ruler gives the best results. If they wish, instead of drawing lines, they may draw curvey "squiggles." When most of the paper is covered with lines, the children may use crayons to fill in the different areas.

This activity will probably take more time than a few minutes. The sheets may be saved for free time later. The children can use the finished sheets for book covers, for covering boxes, or for wrapping gifts.

Descriptions

One child describes an object as well as he can, without telling the name of the object. The others attempt to draw it.

Nutty Representations

Draw a design on the board. Ask the children to guess what it represents. The child who guesses correctly then draws a design that he has invented.

Example: 〰〰 may represent teeth chomping or a zipper.

Stars

Have the children draw a star in the center of a piece of white paper. Color it vividly. Continue drawing one star around another, using different colored crayons.

Community Drawings

Each child starts a drawing on his own piece of paper. After approximately ten seconds, have the children pass their papers to the child sitting next to them. Repeat this procedure until the drawings look fairly complete. You may either let the children have free choice, or assign a certain event or historical period or area currently being studied. The pictures, when completed, make good bulletin board displays.

Pencil Coloring

Draw a picture on the board. With a piece of white chalk, illustrate the various effects of alternating the pressure on the chalk. Explain that the same principle will work with the children's pencils. Tell them to draw a picture of whatever they wish and to color each part using different pressures on the pencil. Still-life pictures such as a bowl of fruit or flowers are excellent for this activity.

Fancy Lettering

Instruct each child to write or print his name in large letters, preferably on a sheet of unlined paper. The child should write his name a second time in the same style, about 1/4″ above the first name. Any loose parallel lines should be connected with small vertical lines. A different design may be drawn within each letter, and if time permits, the finished name colored.

Animal Drawings

Ask the children to draw an animal. The main part of the body may be a heart, a square, a circle, or a triangle.

Plain Old Fun Games

I'm Thinking of a Person

One child comes to the front of the class and declares "I'm thinking of a person." The class asks questions that can only be answered with a "yes" or "no." Questions asked may be, "Is it a man?" "Is it a girl?" "Is he old?" "Is she alive?" "Is she sitting in this room?" "Is he famous?" When a child guesses who it is, then he may think of a person.

Name That Tune!

A child sings the first several notes of a popular song. The first child who guesses the song correctly then becomes the song leader.

Rhythm

The children clap their hands twice and snap first the right fingers and then the left, once each. This should be done in unison. When nearly the whole class has the beat, the teacher names a topic such as "cars." Each child takes a turn naming a car, but the car make must be named while the fingers are snapped, and in rhythm. Any topics may be used, such as names of countries, songs, or cities. When two children miss in a row, a new category should be started.

Exercises

When the class is restless, let a child lead the class in simple exercises, such as jumping jacks, touching toes, deep knee bends, or jogging in place. Everyone will feel more relaxed afterward.

Let's Go Swimming

A teacher demonstration of the following activities will enhance the accuracy of the swimming strokes. The children may "bob" fifty times (stand and do semi-knee bends with arms straight out—waving up and down); do the crawl (use arms for swimming motion while turning the face to the side then looking toward the floor, each to a count of three); or the elementary backstroke (bring hands up under arms and one foot up to the knee, then move arms and leg out to side and down).

Yoga

Press hands together, with palms facing each other. Elbows and forearms should be held in a straight line, away from the body. Press with all strength, and release slowly. Relax. As an alternative, clasp hands and pull the fingers away from each other, then release and repeat.

For relaxation, have children lie on floor and relax each limb, beginning with the feet and continuing up the entire body. Close the eyes for a few minutes, trying not to move any muscles. Girls may not want to lie down so they may just lean over, arms dangling over their head, placing all their weight on the balls of their feet.

Simple Simon

The leader stands at the front of the room. He does different actions such as clapping or jumping. If he says, "Simple Simon says do this," the children must imitate the action. But if he merely says, "Do this," the children are supposed to continue with the previous action instead of imitating the action which corresponded with "Do this." A child who does the action when he is not supposed to must sit down.

The last child to remain standing is the winner and next Simple Simon.

7-Up

Pick seven children to stand in front of the room. The leader says, "Heads down," at which point the other children put their heads on their desks, hiding their eyes. The seven children tiptoe around the room. Each roaming child lightly taps one seated child. When the seven have returned to the front of the room, the leader says, "Stand up if you were tapped." He then asks each standing child who he thinks picked him. If the picked child guesses correctly, he becomes one of the seven to walk around and pick someone, and the child who was "up" initially sits down. To make the game a little more difficult, ask one child to only *pretend* to pick someone.

Fussy, Not Strange

Tell the class that you know an old lady who is "fussy but not strange. She likes beets, but she doesn't like beans. She likes pepper, but she doesn't like salt. She likes Molly, but she doesn't like Susan." Continue until someone catches on and joins in, disclosing what the old lady likes or doesn't like. (Everything the old lady likes must have double letters.)

Lion Hunt

Sit in front of the class and explain that the whole class is going on a lion hunt. The children must repeat everything that you say, while they are imitating your actions. These may be invented and varied.

Some things you might say and do are: "Let's start walking." (You hit your legs with alternate hands.) "Let's cross this bridge." (Tap your feet on the floor.) "We're going through a marsh now." (Make a swishing sound and pretend to push tall grass away from you.) "We'll need to climb this tree to see ahead." (Place one hand on top of another while gradually raising your body.) All these motions are executed on the way to the lion's cave. After a while, you reach the cave. Then point and (stuttering) say quietly, "I see two eyes (pause), a nose (pause), and a m-m-mouth! Let's get out of here!" You then repeat the same motions you used to get to the cave, accelerating the speed to three times as fast. Upon finishing, wipe your brow and say "Phew! That was a close one!"

Huckle Buckle Beanstalk

A group of four or five children leave the room or cover their eyes while one child hides a designated object (a bell, an eraser). He then returns to his seat. The children enter the room (or raise their heads) and proceed to look for the object. When one person discovers the object, he returns nonchalantly to his seat and says, "Huckle Buckle Beanstalk." After all the children looking have discovered the object and returned to their seats, the child who saw it first can hide the object.

A variation of this game may be played in which only one child leaves the room (or hides his eyes). The object is hidden so that a small part of it is visible. When the child returns, the others give him clues by clapping louder if he is close to the object, and softer when he is walking away from it. When the object is found, the child who has found it appoints another child to leave the room, and another to hide the object.

Who's Missing

One child hides his eyes. Another child leaves the classroom while all the children (except the one hiding his eyes) change seats with one another. Then the child who hasn't been looking tries to guess who has left the classroom. If he guesses correctly, he appoints the next person to cover his eyes. If he does not guess correctly, he must hide his eyes again. This is not an easy game.

Eraser Tag

All are seated except two children who are picked to balance erasers on their heads. Starting from different areas of the room, one is designated to catch the other. They must move with their hands behind their backs, (so they do not touch the eraser), and without dropping the eraser. After one is caught, the teacher chooses two new contestants.

The Picnic

Announce to the class, "I'm going on a picnic and taking _____ along." Name an item that begins with the first letter of your last name. For example, if your last name is "Wells," you could say, "My sister Susie Wells is coming and bringing watermelon," or "My friend Mrs. Clark is bringing corn." Continue until most of the children discover the technique and can participate.

Views On News

When the children are particularly restless or tired, it is sometimes a good idea to start an interesting discussion. Many news items and events relevant to our changing times can stimulate children's imagination and interest. The more informed the children are when still open to new ideas, the better able they will one day be to contribute to society.

You might introduce the various topics with a motivational question which requires the children to think. By following each question with a "Why" or "Why not," the discussions can stimulate further interest.

The topics discussed can lend themselves to social studies units. Each question should be conducive to various creative activities in group reporting, writing poems and stories, keeping current events notebooks and bulletin boards, dramatic improvisation, art projects, and class trips.

Some questions that might be asked are:

1. Do you feel that man should continue to explore outer space?

2. Do you think we should send another man to the moon?

3. Experts say that in the future (within fifty or a hundred years) there will not be enough living space for all the people in the world if our population continues to grow at the same fast rate. What do you think the government should do about it?

4. How can we help keep America beautiful? What can we do in our homes, in our schools and in our towns or cities?

5. Do you think cars should be banned from city streets during business hours?

6. Can you think of reasons why it is important to save animals such as alligators, cougars, and wolves that prey on other animals? (This discussion should bring out the importance of these animals in ecological balance: alligators make pools which conserve water and keep other species alive in time of drought; cougars and wolves keep down deer and elk population which destroy trees and grazing lands.)

7. Do you think health care and medicine in America should be free for everyone, no matter what his age?

8. How could we inform more people about job and job-training chances so that every person who wished to work could do so?

9. Would you like to have telephones with television attached so that you could see the person with whom you are talking?

10. What new inventions would you like to see?